I KNOW AMERICA

Our National Capital

Richard Steins

THE MILLBROOK PRESS
Brookfield, Connecticut

Published by The Millbrook Press
2 Old New Milford Road
Brookfield, CT 06804
© 1994 Blackbirch Graphics, Inc.

5 4 3 2 1

Created and produced in association with Blackbirch Graphics.
Series Editor: Tanya Lee Stone

Library of Congress Cataloging-in-Publication Data
Steins, Richard.
    Our national capital / by Richard Steins.
        p.   cm. — (I know America)
    Includes bibliographical references and index.
    Summary: Tells the story of our capital—beginning with L'Enfant's plan and
describes the District's unique position as a center for U.S. politics, history, and
culture.
    ISBN 1-56294-439-8 (lib. bdg.)
    1. Washington (D.C.)—History—Juvenile literature. 2. Washington (D.C.)—
Guidebooks—Juvenile literature. [1. Washington (D.C.)—History. 2. Washington
(D.C.)—Guides.] I. Title. II. Series.
    F194.3.S74   1994
    975.3—dc20   93-38339
                                                                            CIP
                                                                            AC

Acknowledgments and Photo Credits

Cover, pp. 6, 13, 15 (bottom): ©Blackbirch Press; p. 5: AP/Wide World
Photos; pp. 8, 9, 10, 15 (top): Library of Congress; pp. 14, 19, 26, 32, 42:
William Clark/National Park Service; p. 16: Jeff Gnass Photography, Inc;
pp. 21, 24, 27, 34, 38, 40, 44: Photos courtesy of the Washington, D. C.
Convention & Visitors Association; p. 20: Cecil W. Stoughton/U. S.
Department of Interior; p. 23: Frank Senyk; p. 28: B. Markel/Gamma-
Liaison; p. 30: Woodbridge Williams/National Park Service; p. 31: Clare C.
Ralston/National Park Service; pp. 33, 36: National Park Service; p. 43: Leo
de Wys, Inc.

CONTENTS

Washington, D.C., is the capital city of the United States. The "D.C." stands for District of Columbia. The city is bordered on the west and south by the state of Virginia, and on the north and east by the state of Maryland. Washington is a special city—it is not part of any state but is a separate, self-governing district under the supervision of the federal government.

Washington is known mainly as the political center of the United States—and of the world. Since 1800, it has been the home of the three main branches of American government—the presidency, the Congress, and the Supreme Court.

To people everywhere, Washington represents the United States. The embassies of all the countries with which the United States has relations are located

there. As the capital city of the world's greatest democracy, Washington is a symbol of America's heritage. The city is the site of a variety of monuments to past leaders and of historic buildings, many of which are still being used today. In addition, Washington's many museums contain huge collections of art and other items from America's past and from world history.

The Washington of today looks very different than it did two hundred years ago. At that time, the site of the future capital of the United States was a hot, swampy lowland on the Potomac River. Because of the heat, mosquitoes, and diseases, few people lived in the area. Where visitors now walk along broad avenues and tree-lined streets, pigs and chickens roamed freely along the roads. Even as late as the early 1900s, Washington seemed more like a small southern city than a national capital.

But as the nation grew, so did its capital. Today, the beautiful and exciting city of Washington is a true international city.

The Capitol building is an important symbol for the city of Washington, D.C. This inside view of the Capitol shows the dome, which required nine million pounds of cast iron to build.

CHAPTER

1

BUILDING OUR NATIONAL CAPITAL

When George Washington became the first president of the United States on April 30, 1789, he took the oath of office in New York City. New York was at that time the temporary capital of the United States.

The founders of the country wanted to build a new capital as early as the 1780s. However, no one in government could agree on the location. The northern states wanted the capital in their area of the country. The southern states thought the new city should be in the South.

Finally, in 1790, a compromise was reached. The capital would be moved to the upper part of the South—on territory given by the states of Virginia and Maryland. In return, the southern states agreed to let the federal government pay off the states' debts from the Revolution.

Opposite:
George Washington was responsible for picking the site of our nation's capital.

st Branch of
omac R. Washington

A watercolor done in 1831 by artist Augustus Kollner illustrates the beauty of the Potomac River.

President George Washington was given the honor of choosing the location of the new capital. He selected a plot of land along the Potomac River—the location of the city that is now named in his honor.

The Early City Plan

The city of Washington was planned by Pierre Charles L'Enfant. He was born in France in 1754, but came to America as a young man and fought in the American Revolution. In 1791, George Washington asked L'Enfant to plan the nation's new capital. The city's boundaries also needed to be determined at this time. Benjamin Banneker, an African-American scientist and mathematician, assisted in this task.

The major focus of L'Enfant's design was a huge avenue more than a mile long. On one end of the avenue would be the "house of Congress" (now the U.S. Capitol building). On the other end would be the "President's palace" (now the White House). The avenue would be lined with trees. L'Enfant hoped to create a city that would be, as he told Washington, "magnificent enough to grace a great nation."

Unfortunately, L'Enfant had difficulty getting along with the people he needed to work with—especially officials in the government. He was fired in 1792. The building of the new city was continued over the years by other architects.

In 1792, a contest was held for the design of a new building to house the U.S. Congress. The contest was won by William Thornton, who was a medical doctor and an amateur architect. In 1793, the cornerstone of what would become the U.S. Capitol building was laid—on the hill that L'Enfant had chosen as its site. By 1800, the north wing of the new Capitol was ready, and Congress moved from Philadelphia to Washington, D.C. Philadelphia had been

This map of L'Enfant's design for the capital city was published on the front page of a 1792 magazine.

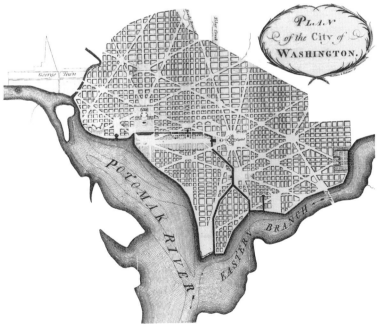

William Thornton won the 1792 contest to design the Capitol building.

the nation's capital throughout most of the Revolutionary War (1775-1783) and the years following, except for the period from 1785 to 1790, when New York City served as the capital.

A contest was also held for a design of the president's new home. The contest was won by an Irish immigrant named James Hoban. The cornerstone of the White House was laid in 1792, but the building was not ready for anyone to move in until the end of 1800. The first residents were President John Adams and his wife, Abigail. Because the laundry yard had not yet been built, Mrs. Adams had to hang her laundry to dry in the White House's huge reception hall, now called the East Room.

Over the next few years, Washington, D.C., grew slowly. In 1803, only about eight thousand people lived there. Most government officials hated Washington. Pennsylvania Avenue, L'Enfant's grand boulevard between the Capitol and the White House, remained a muddy swamp cluttered with people, carriages, horses, pigs, chickens, and garbage. In the summer, the city was hot and humid. Mosquitoes swarmed about in the millions, spreading deadly diseases like malaria. During the summer months, most government leaders fled the city. Congress went into recess, and the president left for his home state, where he stayed until the weather became cooler and it was safe to return. President Thomas Jefferson, for example, spent every summer of his presidency at his home, Monticello, in the cool hills of Virginia.

BENJAMIN BANNEKER

In 1790 and 1791, when the city of Washington, D.C., was still being planned, nearly every African American who lived in the region of the Potomac River was a slave. Yet, the team of architects, engineers, and surveyors who designed the new capital city had one notable black member, Benjamin Banneker. As both a highly respected scientist and mathematician, Banneker had been asked by Thomas Jefferson to be "one of our chief directors in laying out the new Federal City on the Potomac."

Banneker was born in 1731 of free parents in Ellicott, Maryland, and managed to receive the equivalent of an eighth-grade education. (This was more education than most whites received at the time.)

By the mid-1770s, Banneker was established in Maryland as a successful tobacco farmer. He supported both himself and his widowed mother and often spent his free time playing the flute and violin. In 1789, George Ellicott—of the family that founded many towns in the Maryland region—lent Banneker some mathematical texts and astronomical instruments. Without any guidance, Banneker studied and mastered these tools. A year later, he amazed other scientists by developing an almanac of scientific information based on his calculations and investigations.

News of Banneker's talents had reached President Jefferson through various members of the Ellicott family. In 1791, when it came time to put together a team for the planning and building of a new capital city, Benjamin Banneker was asked to help.

Banneker was assigned to serve as scientific assistant to Major Andrew Ellicott, who was in charge of surveying the proposed site for the 10-square-mile city. The two worked closely with Pierre L'Enfant, chief architect of the project.

Halfway through the planning process, L'Enfant was dismissed. He stormed off, taking his plans with him. Banneker, using his own incredible memory and skill, was able to reconstruct the plans for the city of Washington, D.C. He died in 1806, a little-known contributor to our nation's capital.

The New City Burns—and Rebuilds

On the night of August 24, 1814, two years after the British and Americans began fighting in the War of 1812, a British force came ashore in Chesapeake Bay not far from Washington. Within hours the troops attacked the city and set fire to the White House, the Capitol, and many other public buildings.

Before fleeing the White House, First Lady Dolley Madison saved many famous pieces of art. One was a portrait of George Washington by Gilbert Stuart, which hangs today in the White House.

The night of August 24 was stormy and rainy and, because of the weather, the fires set by the British troops did not spread far. But the White House and Capitol were severely damaged, and President and Mrs. Madison were forced to move to Octagon House. Work on the damaged Capitol building was not completely finished until 1830. The rest of the city quickly recovered from the war damage and by 1822 Washington's population had risen to more than 15,000.

The Civil War and After

During the Civil War (1861-1865) and the years that followed, many changes occurred in Washington, D.C. While the North (the Union) fought the South (the Confederacy), thousands of Union troops were stationed in the capital, which was in constant danger of being attacked. In 1861, Northern troops camped on the White House lawn, partly to protect President

MOUNT VERNON

Not far from the city of Washington is Mount Vernon, the home of George Washington, the first president of the United States. It stands high on a hill in Virginia, overlooking the Potomac River.

The land on which Mount Vernon is built came into the Washington family in 1674. At the time that George Washington lived there, this plantation consisted of more than eight thousand acres. Today, only five hundred acres remain.

Washington loved the many pathways and trees on his estate, and the entrance to Mount Vernon is still lined with trees that Washington himself planted in the late 1700s.

During the forty-five years that George Washington owned Mount Vernon, he took great interest in enlarging and improving it. Washington spent time away from the mansion during wartime and during his presidency. At the end of his second term as president, however, Washington returned to the estate and remained there until his death two years later.

George Washington and his wife, Martha, are buried on the grounds of Mount Vernon, in a huge tomb that contains the remains of more than twenty other members of the Washington family. Nearby is a special cemetery containing the bodies of the slaves who served the Washington family. Memorial services are held each February at Washington's grave to celebrate the birthday of the nation's first president.

Mount Vernon was almost lost as a national shrine. Washington's descendants owned the estate until the late 1850s because neither the federal government nor the state of Virginia would buy the property when it was offered for sale. Then, in 1858, a group of private citizens purchased Mount Vernon, which was in danger of collapsing. It was restored to its original appearance and today hosts visitors from all over the world.

MOST HALLOWED GROUND

Directly across the Potomac River from Washington is Arlington National Cemetery. It is located in Virginia on 612 hilly acres overlooking the city. Thousands of soldiers and many famous Americans, including former presidents William Howard Taft and John F. Kennedy, are buried there.

The cemetery was founded during the Civil War on the grounds of the former home of Confederate general Robert E. Lee. In 1863, the young son of the U.S. quartermaster general Montgomery Meigs was killed in battle. Meigs was grief-stricken and angry. In his sorrow he decided to honor his son and other Union soldiers who had died. At the same time, he wanted to make sure that Robert E. Lee could never return to his home on the hill.

Meigs turned two hundred acres of Lee's front yard into a cemetery for Union soldiers. If Robert E. Lee had any idea of living in his old house, he would be forced to look out his front window and see the graves of thousands of soldiers who had died fighting against the South.

Probably the most-visited site in Arlington is the Tomb of the Unknowns, a seventy-nine-ton white marble block containing the unidentified remains of soldiers from every war the United States fought in—from World War I to the Persian Gulf War. The tomb is guarded day and night by soldiers. Each year on Veterans Day (November 11), the president of the United States places a floral wreath at the tomb to honor all Americans who died defending their country.

Abraham Lincoln and partly because there was no place else to go. The Capitol building served as a temporary troop barracks and hospital.

Despite the growth of the war years, Washington, D.C., remained backward in many areas. It was not until 1871 that plans were made to pave the streets (including Pennsylvania Avenue), build sewers, and add gas lights to parts of the city that had no lighting. During the 1870s, thousands of trees were also planted, giving Washington its current appearance as a city of parks, lawns, and trees.

The next great period of change occurred in the early 1900s, with the creation of Washington's Mall. The Mall is a vast, rectangular-shaped park that extends from the grounds of the Capitol building to the grounds of the Washington Monument. L'Enfant had planned such a large park in his original design, but the site of the Mall remained covered with private houses, junkyards, and railroad tracks until after 1900.

When the park was finally created according to Pierre L'Enfant's original plan, it included the first Smithsonian Institution building, a red structure often called "The Castle." Eventually the Washington, Jefferson, and Lincoln memorials and the Vietnam Veterans Memorial were also built there. It has been the site of such historic events as the 1963 civil rights march on Washington led by Martin Luther King, Jr.

Today, Washington, D.C., is home to about 600,000 people, many of whom work for the federal government.

Above:
A view of Washington, D.C., drawn before the Mall was completed.

Below:
A current photograph of the same view showing part of the Mall.

C H A P T E R

2

THE SEAT OF GOVERNMENT

Washington, D.C., is one of the few cities in the world that was established for the sole purpose of being the country's seat of government. All major offices of the American government are within the city.

The President, Congress, and the Supreme Court

The president lives with his family in the 132-room White House, which has been the home of every U.S. president since 1800. The White House, at 1600 Pennsylvania Avenue, is a private residence, an office, and a public building. On certain days of the week, tourists are permitted to visit the large reception rooms on the first floor. The second floor, where the president and his family live, is not open to the public.

Opposite:
A view of the White House from the South lawn.

Opposite:
The Capitol building's Statue of Freedom was taken down and restored in September 1993. It was returned to its place on top of the dome by helicopter.

Every day, seven days a week, hundreds of people arrive at the White House to work. They are the people who assist the president in running the executive branch of government.

Over the years, major changes and repairs have been made to the White House. Between 1948 and 1952, during the last few years of Harry Truman's presidency, the inside was completely rebuilt. In the early 1960s, Jacqueline Kennedy, the president's wife, redecorated the rooms. The most recent repair work was done in 1989. At that time, the paint on the outside of the White House was stripped. While removing the old paint, fifty layers thick in some places, workers found burn marks from the 1814 fire.

Congress is the branch of government that makes and passes laws. It meets in the Capitol building at the other end of Pennsylvania Avenue. The 435 members of the House of Representatives sit in one wing, and the 100 senators sit in another. These wings were added to the original building between 1851 and 1865.

At the top of the Capitol building there is a 285-foot-high dome topped by the Statue of Freedom. Surrounding the dome are thirty-six columns. The Statue of Freedom was positioned on top of the dome in 1863. The rotunda beneath the dome contains numerous statues and paintings of American statesmen. In the center of the rotunda is a marble disk that marks the spot where the coffins of many American presidents have been placed on public view

prior to burial. The Capitol is also the site of National Statuary Hall, a room with many statues of famous world leaders.

The Supreme Court used to meet in part of the Capitol building. It did not have a building of its own until 1935, when a structure designed to look like a grand Greek temple was opened. Visitors to the Supreme Court walk up a wide flight of marble steps to the entrance of the building, over which are carved the words "Equal Justice Under Law." These words reflect the Supreme Court's main job—to make sure that laws passed by state and other local governments are fair in terms of the U.S. Constitution.

The Supreme Court is the highest court in the United States.

The Department of Defense

Many of Washington's major offices are not within the limits of the District of Columbia. One of the largest government divisions is the Department of Defense, located across the Potomac River in Virginia. The Defense Department's building is called the Pentagon. It is a five-sided structure with five floors and an inner courtyard of five square miles. The Pentagon was completed in 1943, during World War II.

This view of the Pentagon building shows its five-sided shape and the inner courtyard.

The Pentagon is one of the largest employers in the federal government. More than 23,000 people work in the Pentagon building alone. There they supervise the entire U.S. military—the Army, Air Force, Navy, and Marines.

Washington's Local Government

Unlike any other city or state in the country, Washington, D.C., has always been governed by the federal government. As a result of this, people who live in Washington, D.C., have not always had the same voting opportunities as other Americans.

A CITY OF QUADRANTS

The city of Washington is divided into four unequal sections, called quadrants, with the Capitol building at the center. The four quadrants are defined by North Capitol Street, East Capitol Street, South Capitol Street, and the Mall. The quadrants are labeled like the points found on a compass: Northwest (NW), Northeast (NE), Southeast (SE), and Southwest (SW).

Northwest

The Northwest quadrant is the heart of Washington. Most of the important government buildings, monuments, and museums are located here. Georgetown, a collection of charming neighborhoods filled with brick or cobblestone streets and historic homes, is also located in this quadrant. It is the oldest part of the city and contains many of Washington's finest restaurants and shops.

Southwest

Neighborhoods in the Southwest quadrant are home to many people from different countries. Part of the Mall, a dramatic open space that stretches all the way from the Capitol building to the Washington Monument, also falls within this section.

Southeast

The Capitol building sits in the center of all four quadrants, but most of the adjoining grounds, offices, and apartments fall within the southeast section of the city. Farther south and east, neighborhoods such as Anacostia have been troubled by poverty and crime.

Northeast

This quadrant is filled with many grand and impressive sights. The principal attractions in this area are the National Shrine of the Immaculate Conception (the largest Roman Catholic church in the United States), a Franciscan monastery that houses ancient works of art, and the National Arboretum, which contains more than four hundred acres of flowering plants, trees, and shrubs.

The Twenty-third Amendment to the Constitution was passed in 1961, allowing citizens of Washington to vote in presidential elections for the first time.

In 1967, the city government was expanded to include a mayor-commissioner and a council, appointed by the president and approved by the Senate. Then on May 7, 1974, the Home Rule Charter bill was approved by Congress, giving the citizens of Washington the right to elect their mayor and council. This was the first time since 1871, when Congress governed the District of Columbia, that Washingtonians could vote for their local leaders.

Washington elects one member to the House of Representatives. That person, however, does not have a vote in Congress.

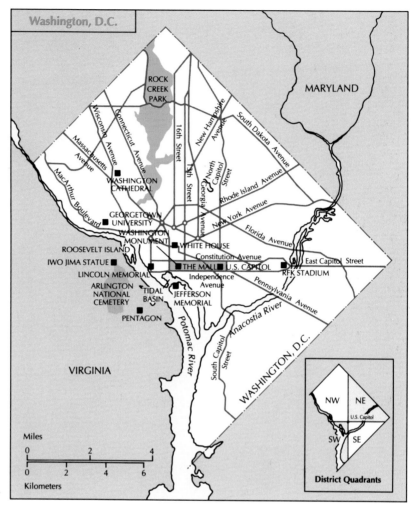

Washington, D.C.

MARYLAND

ROCK CREEK PARK

Wisconsin Avenue

Connecticut Avenue

Massachusetts Avenue

MacArthur Boulevard

16th Street

14th Street

New Hampshire Avenue

North Capitol Street

Georgia Avenue

South Dakota Avenue

Rhode Island Avenue

New York Avenue

Florida Avenue

WASHINGTON CATHEDRAL

GEORGETOWN UNIVERSITY

WASHINGTON MONUMENT

ROOSEVELT ISLAND

IWO JIMA STATUE

LINCOLN MEMORIAL

ARLINGTON NATIONAL CEMETERY

TIDAL BASIN

PENTAGON

WHITE HOUSE

Constitution Avenue

THE MALL

U.S. CAPITOL

East Capitol Street

RFK STADIUM

Independence Avenue

JEFFERSON MEMORIAL

Pennsylvania Avenue

Potomac River

Anacostia River

South Capitol Street

WASHINGTON, D.C.

VIRGINIA

Miles
0   2   4
0   2   4   6
Kilometers

District Quadrants

NW   NE
U.S. Capitol
SW   SE

23

CENTER OF A NATION'S HISTORY

If you walk through the streets of Washington today, you will see all the signs of a modern U.S. city. But there are many differences between Washington and other large cities in America. The first thing a visitor is likely to notice is that Washington has no huge skyscrapers. Over the years, the city's planners decided that Washington must not have tall buildings that block its great monuments. As you approach the city, the most visible sites are the huge Capitol dome and the Washington Monument.

Washington is famous for its large number of museums. There are also many historic buildings, beautifully preserved and still in daily use.

Opposite:
Every year, up to 10 million people from all over the world travel to Washington, D.C., and visit the Capitol building.

The National Archives, located in an area known as the Federal Triangle, is a popular tourist attraction.

Historic Buildings and Museums

The National Archives, on Constitution Avenue just north of the Mall, houses some of the nation's greatest historic treasures. On display for the public to view are the Declaration of Independence, the Constitution, and the Bill of Rights (the first ten amendments to the Constitution). During visiting hours, armed guards stand near these documents to protect them. At night, they are lowered into a huge vault. The current National Archives building was constructed in the 1930s.

The Library of Congress was founded in 1800. It is located on 1st Street, S.E., and is the largest library in the United States. Today it houses more than 27 million books as well as millions of other items, such as the letters of George Washington and collections of musical instruments. The Library of Congress is open to the public for reading and research and is frequently the site of musical concerts. The main Library of Congress building was constructed between 1889 and 1897 and contains elaborate murals, marble floors, and statues.

The Smithsonian Institution is the world's largest museum complex. Millions of visitors each year view its displays of science, history, technology, and culture. Most of its buildings are in Washington, D.C., but a few are located elsewhere in the country.

"The Castle" was the first building to be built for the Smithsonian Institution.

UNITED STATES HOLOCAUST MEMORIAL MUSEUM

The United States Holocaust Memorial Museum was opened in 1993. It honors the more than 6 million people—most of them Jews—who were killed in concentration camps during World War II by a group of Germans called Nazis.

The museum is located on Raoul Wallenberg Place, near Independence Avenue. Its brick interior was designed to remind people of a concentration camp. Inside the four-story building are exhibits that bring to life the experiences of those 6 million people whom the Nazis rounded up throughout Europe in the late 1930s and early 1940s and transported to concentration camps, where many were killed in gas chambers. This mass

The museum celebrated its opening on April 22, 1993.

murder of human beings has come to be known as "the Holocaust."

Each visitor to the museum is given the identity card of a Holocaust victim who was his or her own age. At any point during the tour, the visitor can place the card in a computer and discover what happened to that person. On the third floor, the walls of the museum get narrower, to symbolize the narrowing choices that Holocaust victims faced. On this floor is also a replica (an object made to look like the original) of the barracks at Auschwitz, one of the worst concentration camps; an actual railroad car used to transport the victims; and a tower containing family photographs of 1,500 people who died in the Holocaust.

The museum also shows videos and displays possessions, such as shoes and clothing, of those who were killed in the concentration camps.

The United States Holocaust Memorial Museum is a living shrine to those who died at the hands of the Nazis and a reminder that people are capable of acts of brutality toward other human beings.

In 1829, an English scientist named James Smithson left a large sum of money in his will to the American government. The money was to be used to set up an organization for "the increase...of knowledge among men." Seventeen years later, in 1846, the Smithsonian Institution was established.

The original Smithsonian building was finished in 1855. It is a red sandstone structure designed to look like a twelfth-century castle. Located on the Mall, it housed a science museum, an art gallery, and research laboratories and was also the private home of the museum's director. Today, "The Castle" is used as the administrative offices of the Smithsonian. Among the most well-known Smithsonian museums are the National Museum of American History, the National Museum of Natural History, the National Air and Space Museum, the National Museum of American Art, the National Portrait Gallery, the Hirshhorn Museum and Sculpture Garden, and the National Museum of African Art.

The National Gallery of Art, on the north side of the Mall, is considered part of the Smithsonian, but it has its own board of directors. It contains one of the world's largest collections of Western painting and sculpture. The National Gallery consists of a West Building, which opened in 1941, and an East Building, which opened in 1978. The buildings are dramatically different in style. The West Building has a dome and a rotunda, while the East Building is very modern.

Historic Memorials

Any visitor to Washington can relive the nation's history by walking along the city's streets. Washington remembers the nation's past through well-known monuments that pay tribute to our distinguished leaders as well as to the thousands of ordinary citizens who gave their lives in the defense of their country.

The Washington Monument stands as a centerpiece in the nation's capital. To the north is the White House, and to the east, across the Mall, is the Capitol building. Pierre L'Enfant had wanted a memorial in honor of George Washington to be built farther to the east on the Mall, but the earth was too soggy. The monument was finally started in 1848 and finished in 1884. It was opened to the public in 1888.

At one point, though, construction was stopped because of a lack of money during the Civil War. The original marble does not match the marble used after building resumed. Standing at its base and looking up, a visitor can see the different colors of stone.

The Washington Monument stands about 555 feet high. The interior is hollow and visitors may climb to the top for a beautiful view of the city.

The Lincoln Memorial, to the west of the Washington Monument and just opposite the Arlington Memorial Bridge, honors America's Civil War president, Abraham Lincoln. The building is designed to look like a Greek temple. Surrounding it are thirty-six columns—one for each state that belonged to the Union at the time Lincoln died. Although many people wanted to build a monument to honor the sixteenth president, the Lincoln Memorial was not dedicated until 1922, fifty-seven years after his death. At the ceremony was Robert Lincoln, the seventy-nine-year-old son of the late president.

Inside the building is a huge stone statue of Lincoln sitting in a chair. This nineteen-foot-high statue was created by the sculptor Daniel Chester French. On the limestone walls are inscribed two of Lincoln's most famous speeches—the Gettysburg Address and his second inaugural address.

An aerial view of the reflecting pool at the Lincoln Memorial, showing the Potomac River in the background.

The Lincoln Memorial has been the site of important events. During the 1963 civil rights march on Washington, Martin Luther King, Jr., delivered his "I Have a Dream" speech from its steps.

In keeping with the spirit of L'Enfant's design, the Lincoln Memorial is perfectly aligned with the Washington Monument and the Capitol. In front of it is a long, narrow body of water called the Reflecting Pool. Standing in front of the Lincoln Memorial at night, you can see a reflection of the Washington Monument and the Capitol in the pool.

The Jefferson Memorial was dedicated and opened to the public in 1943. It honors Thomas Jefferson, the third president of the United States and author of the Declaration of Independence.

The Jefferson Memorial is a round, Roman-style building surrounded by columns. Inside is a large statue of Jefferson. It is directly south of the Washington Monument and looks beyond toward the White House. The memorial was built on land reclaimed from the Potomac River and faces the Tidal Basin, a lake created by engineers.

Selections of Jefferson's writings are inscribed on the interior walls of the Jefferson Memorial.

The Vietnam Veterans Memorial, located near the Lincoln Memorial, is one of the most interesting and moving monuments. It was designed by a young student of architecture named Maya Ying Lin, who submitted her sketches as part of a contest. The Vietnam Veterans Memorial was dedicated in 1982. It consists of two walls that meet on an angle. One wall points toward the Lincoln Memorial; the other points toward the Washington Monument. The walls are made of dark marble that reflects the surrounding trees and grass. On the walls are inscribed the names of more than 58,000 men and women who lost their lives in the Vietnam War during the 1960s and 1970s.

The capital city was the site of many anti-Vietnam War protests and demonstrations during the 1960s and 1970s and is now the location of the Vietnam Veterans Memorial.

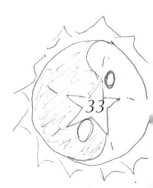

33

CHAPTER

4

A PLACE TO ENJOY

Although Washington is a city of politics and history, it is also an entertaining city. Visitors and residents can find all forms of amusement. There are theaters, parks, museums, concert halls, a sports stadium, and many other interesting places.

Much of Washington, D.C.'s, cultural life was developed in the twentieth century. Prior to then, the city's principal interest was government and politics—something that many of its residents disliked. Today, however, Washington has become a leading cultural capital.

John F. Kennedy Center for the Performing Arts

At the center of Washington's cultural life is the John F. Kennedy Center for the Performing Arts, located on seventeen acres along the Potomac River. It was

Opposite:
The John F. Kennedy Center for the Performing Arts was created as a memorial to the assassinated president. The center celebrated its opening with the world premier of Leonard Bernstein's Mass.

35

WHITE HOUSE EASTER-EGG ROLL

One of the most popular Washington events for children under the age of eight is the Easter-Egg Roll. It takes place every year on Easter Monday on the lawn of the White House and is open to anyone who wishes to attend.

During this gathering, children from all over the country take part in a hunt for more than a thousand wooden eggs that are hidden all over the White House grounds. Many of the eggs have been signed by the president and the First Lady and by other famous people. There is also an egg-rolling contest as well as storytelling and entertainment by clowns, magicians, and acrobats.

The first Easter-Egg Roll took place in 1878, when Rutherford B. Hayes was president.

opened in 1971, and is named after the thirty-fifth president of the United States, who was killed by an assassin in 1963. As a performing arts complex, the Kennedy Center is the home of a number of cultural organizations. The largest and most well known are the National Symphony Orchestra, the Washington Opera, and the Washington Ballet. The complex also includes a movie theater and stage theaters where plays are performed.

Within the Kennedy Center are gifts from forty different nations. An exhibit hall displays the flag of every country with which the United States is on friendly terms.

Theaters

The National Theater on Pennsylvania Avenue is the oldest theater in Washington. It was established in 1835 and completely renovated in 1983. Because it is so large, the National Theater often presents Broadway musicals.

The Arena Stage, on 6th Street, has been in operation for more than fifty years. It is the nation's oldest ensemble company. (An "ensemble" is a group of actors who perform many different plays.) Inside the Arena building are three stages, which allow more than one play to be performed at a time.

Ford's Theatre, on 10th Street, N.W., was opened in 1863 and is the most famous theater in Washington. It was in this theater that Abraham Lincoln was assassinated. On the evening of April 14,

Ford's Theatre,
where Abraham
Lincoln was
assassinated in
1865.

1865, the president and his wife were attending a performance of a play called *Our American Cousin,* when the actor John Wilkes Booth sneaked into the president's box and shot him in the head.

After the assassination, Ford's Theatre was closed by order of the government. Later, in the 1890s, it was used for government offices. Then, in 1968, after being restored to its original appearance, it was reopened to the public as a 740-seat theater with a museum in the basement. On display are the clothes that the president was wearing when he was killed, the pistol that was used to shoot him, and other items from Lincoln's life.

Museums

The Corcoran Gallery of Art, near the White House, was founded in 1859 as Washington's first art museum. In 1897, it was moved to a different building. The museum was named after William Wilson Corcoran, a Washington banker and art collector. He donated the money to set up the gallery and left his large collection of paintings to the museum. The Corcoran is famous for its many paintings by great American artists, but it also has a collection by well-known Europeans.

The Capital Children's Museum, on 3rd Street, N.E., is unlike most museums in that it allows children to touch the works on display. Visitors can play with special-effects television equipment and computers and operate an old-fashioned switchboard. A copy of a 30,000-year-old cave allows children to explore what life was like millions of years ago.

The Folger Shakespeare Library, on East Capitol Street, S.E., is as much a museum as it is a library. In 1930, Henry Clay Folger and his wife, Emily, donated their collection of Shakespeare books to the public. Two years later, in 1932, the building housing this collection was completed. The Folger Shakespeare Library proudly displays the largest collection of Shakespeare material. In addition to the Folgers' collection, the building contains a small theater where concerts and readings of Shakespeare's works are given. The grounds of the library contain a garden with plants and herbs typical of Shakespeare's time.

THE NATIONAL ZOOLOGICAL PARK

The National Zoological Park, founded by the Smithsonian Institution in 1890, is located next to Rock Creek Park and contains more than 5,000 animals. For many years, its star attractions were the famous pandas Hsing-Hsing and Ling-Ling, which were gifts from China to the United States. A rare white Bengal tiger is another popular feature, along with the many small mammals that are part of the collection.

Within the zoo's more than 170 acres is a large glass-domed building known as Amazonia. This 15,000-square-foot exhibit building features fish and plants from the Amazon River regions of South America. A cascading tropical river contains many unusual fish, and a rain forest features 358 species of exotic plants and dozens of animals. A biologist's field station allows children to learn about how nature is studied.

Other notable attractions and displays at the National Zoo include the spectacular Great Flight Cage, in which people can walk among birds of many sizes, shapes, and colors. Zoolab is a learning center, where hands-on activities and special displays offer the curious a chance to learn more about the natural world.

With its many unusual and interesting attractions, the National Zoo is considered one of the finest in the United States and one of the best in the world.

Other Attractions

The Robert F. Kennedy Memorial Stadium, on East Capitol Street, was named in honor of the U.S. attorney general and New York senator who was assassinated in 1968. The main stadium has 50,000 seats and is the home of the Washington Redskins. It is also used for rodeos, circuses, and other sporting events such as boxing and wrestling.

The J. Edgar Hoover Building (FBI Building), which takes up an entire city block, is the headquarters of the Federal Bureau of Investigation. The five thousand people who visit it daily are treated to dramatic presentations of the FBI's most famous cases. They can also see exhibits dealing with FBI activities in organized crime and bank robberies.

The Washington National Cathedral (Cathedral Church of St. Peter and St. Paul) is an Episcopal church. It is often called "the last of the great cathedrals" because it was built by hand, stone by stone, without the use of steel supports or any machinery. In the shape of a cross, it is about 530 feet long and seats four thousand people. It was under construction from 1970 until 1990.

The Octagon House, completed in 1800 for a family named Taylor, has only six sides, not eight, as its name (Octagon) indicates. President Madison and his wife lived there for a while in 1814 after the White House was burned. Today, it is the headquarters of the American Institute of Architects and is open to the public for tours.

NATIONAL TREE-LIGHTING CEREMONY

Most tourists visit Washington during the spring and summer. For those visiting in the winter, one of the most popular events is the national tree-lighting ceremony.

Every year, a huge Christmas tree is selected from somewhere in the United States and brought to Washington. It is then placed on the south grounds of the White House, where it is decorated and hung with lights.

When the tree is ready, the president and his family press a button, and the tree instantly lights up. This opens the Christmas season in Washington and serves to symbolize the nation's commitment to the spirit of the holidays.

The Frederick Douglass Home was named for a leader in the movement to free the slaves. Douglass lived in this house from 1877 to 1895. It has been preserved in his memory and contains many items from his life. It is open for tours.

The Doll's House and Toy Museum of Washington contains dolls, dollhouses, doll furnishings, a toy shop, and an ice cream parlor for birthday parties.

Parks and Nature Centers

Washington is a "green" city. It is covered with many small and large parks.

Potomac Park, a 720-acre expanse on the Tidal Basin, is one of the most popular parks in Washington. West Potomac Park is the site of the annual Cherry Blossom Festival; East Potomac Park is a wooded area where people jog, picnic, and play tennis.

Rock Creek Park, with its 1,750 acres, extends from the Potomac River in Washington 12 miles north to the Maryland border. Within the park are playgrounds, woods, hiking trails, a nature center, a golf course, and a center for horseback riding.

The U.S. Botanic Garden, on 1st Street, S.W., contains collections of plants from all over the world. It was founded in 1820 and is now housed in a series of buildings made of glass and stone. The

Thousands of people travel to Washington, D.C., every year to see the cherry blossoms in full bloom.

THE CHERRY BLOSSOM FESTIVAL

One of the most well-known events in Washington occurs every April, when more than 1,300 Japanese

The Cherry Blossom Festival parade.

cherry blossom trees located near the Tidal Basin in Potomac Park come into bloom.

The Cherry Blossom Festival is a week-long celebration with parades, entertainment, and parties. The highlight is the lighting of a three-hundred-year-old Japanese lantern, which was given to the people of Washington by the governor of Tokyo in 1954.

The Cherry Blossom Festival draws thousands of tourists to Washington every spring. When these trees are in full bloom, the shore of the Tidal Basin is filled with the pink and white colors of the cherry blossoms.

Botanic Garden overlooks the Reflecting Pool near the Lincoln Memorial. On its grounds are a park with a rose garden and many wooded areas where visitors can sit and relax.

The United States National Arboretum consists of 425 acres covered with trees, shrubs, and flowers from all over the world. Among the arboretum's special features are a garden of Japanese miniature trees (donated in 1976), a bird garden featuring shrubs that attract birds, and an "American Garden" containing grasses found throughout the United States.

Chronology

1790 George Washington selects a site on the Potomac River for new national capital.

1791 Pierre Charles L'Enfant submits his plans for the new capital.

1792 Construction of the White House begins.

1793 Work begins on the Capitol building.

1800 Congress moves into the Capitol. President and Mrs. Adams move into the White House. The Library of Congress is founded.

1814 The British burn many buildings in Washington, including the Capitol and the White House.

1820 The U.S. Botanic Garden is founded.

1830 Rebuilding of the severely burned Capitol building is completed.

1835 The National Theater is established.

1846 The Smithsonian Institution is established.

1859 The Corcoran Gallery of Art is founded.

1863 Arlington National Cemetery is created on grounds of Robert E. Lee's estate. Ford's Theatre opens.

1865 President Lincoln is assassinated at Ford's Theatre in Washington.

1871 A plan is begun for improving streets and adding sewers and gas lights to Washington. Congress assumes direct control of the District of Columbia.

1884 The Washington Monument is completed but does not open until 1888.

1890 The National Zoological Park is founded.

Early 1900s A plan to develop the Mall is announced.

1922 The Lincoln Memorial is dedicated.

1930s The National Archives Building is built.

1932 The Folger Shakespeare Library opens.

1935 The Supreme Court building opens.

1941 The West Building of the National Gallery of Art opens.

1943 The Jefferson Memorial is dedicated. The Pentagon is built.

1952 Rebuilding of the White House is completed.

1961 Citizens of Washington are granted the right to vote in presidential elections.

1963 Martin Luther King, Jr., leads a civil rights march on Washington.

1971 The John F. Kennedy Center for the Performing Arts opens.
1974 Washington's citizens receive the right to elect their own mayor and council.
1978 The East Building of the National Gallery of Art opens.
1982 The Vietnam Veterans Memorial is dedicated.
1993 The National Holocaust Memorial Museum opens.

For Further Reading

Climo, Shirley. *City! Washington, D.C.* New York: Macmillan, 1991.

Fradin, Dennis B. *Washington, D.C.* Chicago: Childrens Press, 1992.

Hilton, Suzanne. *A Capital Capital City, 1790-1814.* New York: Macmillan, 1992.

Horg, Stan. *Capital for the Nation.* New York: Dutton, 1990.

Krementz, Jill. *A Visit to Washington.* New York: Scholastic, 1987.

Petersen, Anne. *Kidding Around Washington, D.C.: A Young Person's Guide to the City.* Santa Fe, NM: John Muir Publications, 1989.

Index